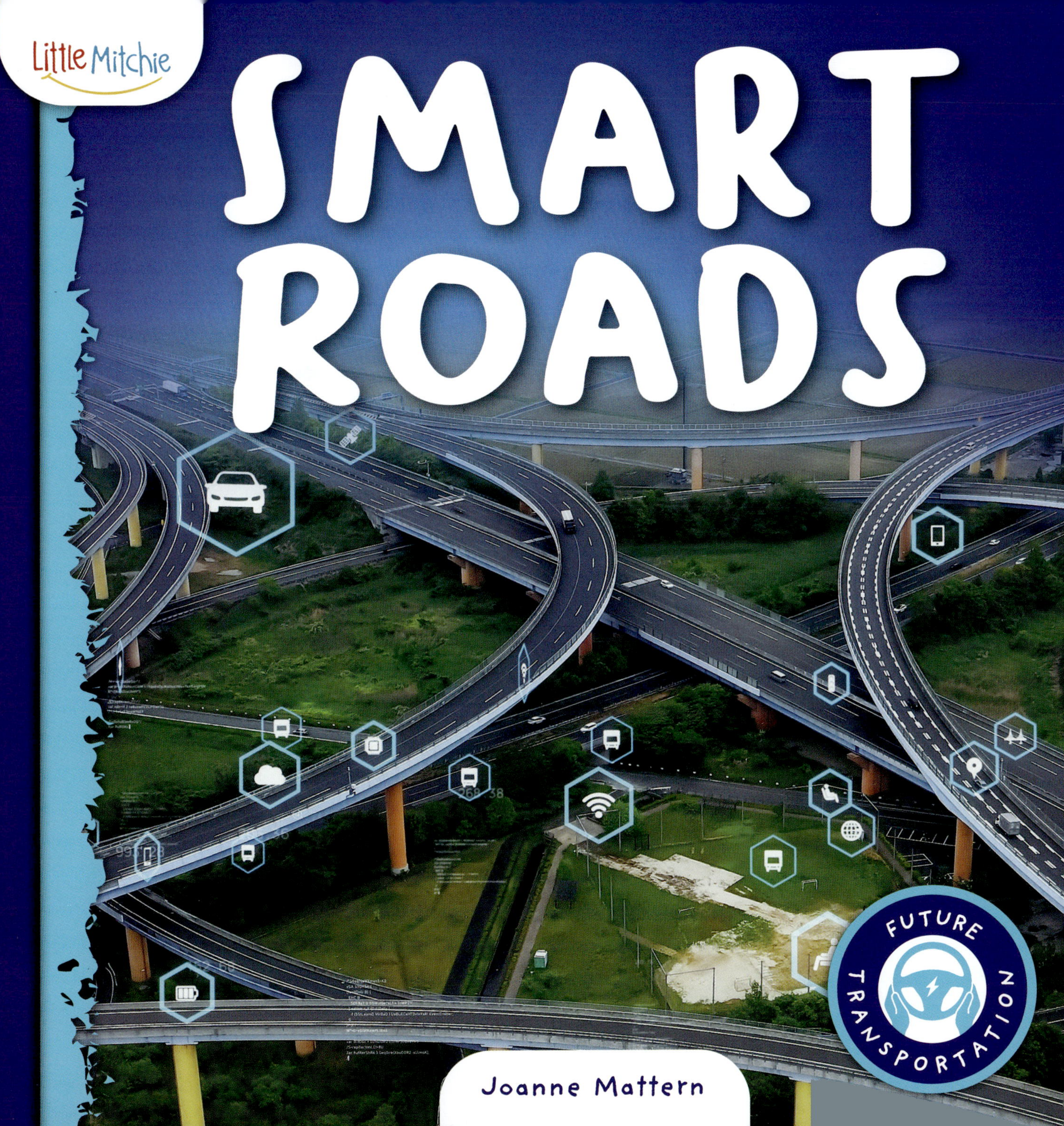
Little Mitchie
SMART ROADS
FUTURE TRANSPORTATION
Joanne Mattern

CREATING YOUNG NONFICTION READERS

Little Mitchie books spark curiosity and support early nonfiction reading for students in Grades 2-3. Designed to build vocabulary, support second language learners, and prepare readers for middle-grade content, each book includes helpful tips for parents and educators to build confidence and deepen understanding of the world.

TIPS FOR READING NONFICTION WITH BEGINNING READERS

Talk about Nonfiction

Begin by explaining that nonfiction books give us information that is true. The book will be organized around a specific topic or idea, and we may learn new facts through reading.

Look at the Parts

Most nonfiction books have helpful features. Our *Little Mitchie* titles include color photographs and graphic aids, a table of contents, a glossary, and an index. Share the purpose of these features with your reader.

Color Photos and Graphic Aids

A lot of information can be found by "reading" photos, charts, maps, and other graphic aids found within nonfiction texts. Help your reader learn more about the different ways information can be displayed.

Table of Contents

Located at the front of the book, this list shows the big ideas within the text and the page numbers where they can be found.

Glossary

Located at the back of the book, the glossary defines key words and phrases that are related to the topic. These words and phrases can be found in the text in colored type.

Index

Located at the back of the book, an index is an alphabetical list of topics and the page numbers where they can be found.

With a little help and guidance about reading nonfiction, you can feel good about introducing a young reader to the world of *Little Mitchie* nonfiction books.

Little Mitchie is an imprint of:

Mitchell Lane
PUBLISHERS

2001 SW 31st Avenue
Hallandale, FL 33009
mitchelllanepub.com

First Edition, 2027.

Author: Joanne Mattern
Designer: Bobbie Houser
Editor: Tricia Hoffman

Library of Congress Cataloging-in-Publication Data
Names: Name, Author, author.
Title: Smart Roads / by Joanne Mattern

Description: Hallandale, FL :
Mitchell Lane Publishers, [2027]

Identifiers:
ISBN 979-8-89260-871-8 (library bound)
ISBN 979-8-89260-968-5 (eBook)

Library of Congress Control Number: 2026936108

PHOTO CREDITS
Alamy: NurPhoto SRL, 13; Robert Evans, 14; Hemis, 17; monicaodo, 22; Public Domain: Wikipedia, 9; Shutterstock: metamorworks, cover, 1; Around the World Photos, 5; Peter Titmuss, 6; Sugeng Dwi N, 10; knelson20, 11; karelnoppe, 19; metamorworks, 21.

TABLE OF CONTENTS

Chapter One

A DIFFERENT KIND OF ROAD

Tanika and her mother were driving to the store. The traffic light ahead of them turned green as their car got closer. "That was good timing," Tanika said.

"The light knew our car was coming," her mother said. "This is a smart road."

A sign flashed over their heads. "Accident ahead," it read. "Move to right lane." Tanika's mother changed lanes. A police car was already at the accident.

"The road sent a message to the police so they can get there faster," Tanika's mother said. "Smart roads make driving better!"

Chapter Two

SMART ROADS TODAY

In 1939, New York City held a World's Fair. A display called Futurama showed roads that sent out radio **signals**.

In the 1990s, the U.S. government offered money to companies to build smart roads. They wanted to make driving easier and safer.

SEEING THE FUTURE

Futurama was the most popular exhibit at the 1939 New York World's Fair.

Smart roads use **sensors** and cameras to help drivers. Sensors send information to a computer. They tell the computer where there is heavy traffic or if there is bad weather. The computer sends messages to **electronic** signs that drivers can read.

UPDATED INFO

Computers can change the information on an electronic sign to give updated traffic conditions.

Other countries have smart roads too. In the Netherlands, some highways have lane markers that light up when it gets dark to help drivers see where they are going. South Korea has special roads that can charge electric buses while they drive.

ENERGY EFFICIENT

The charging system in South Korea turns on only when it senses electric buses. It doesn't waste energy on regular cars.

Smart roads don't just **communicate** with drivers. They also make changes. Some smart roads have heat panels underneath. If the road senses ice or snow, the panels turn on. They warm up the road and make it safe to drive on.

WIRELESS IS THE KEY

Wireless technology is a big part of smart roads. It lets sensors send messages to each other.

Chapter Three

THE FUTURE OF SMART ROADS

Countries are always looking for new ways to make roads better. France and China are working on making roads covered with **solar panels**. These roads create energy as cars drive on them. The United States is looking into solar roads too.

There are some problems with smart roads. They cost a lot of money to build.

Smart roads also need good technology. Many rely on 5G networks, but these networks don't exist everywhere.

PARTNERS IN DRIVING

Smart roads work best with smart cars. It is likely that self-driving cars will make roads even smarter in the future.

Smart roads have many **features** that can help drivers. They make driving safer, faster, and more fun!

LET'S LOOK AT A SMART ROAD

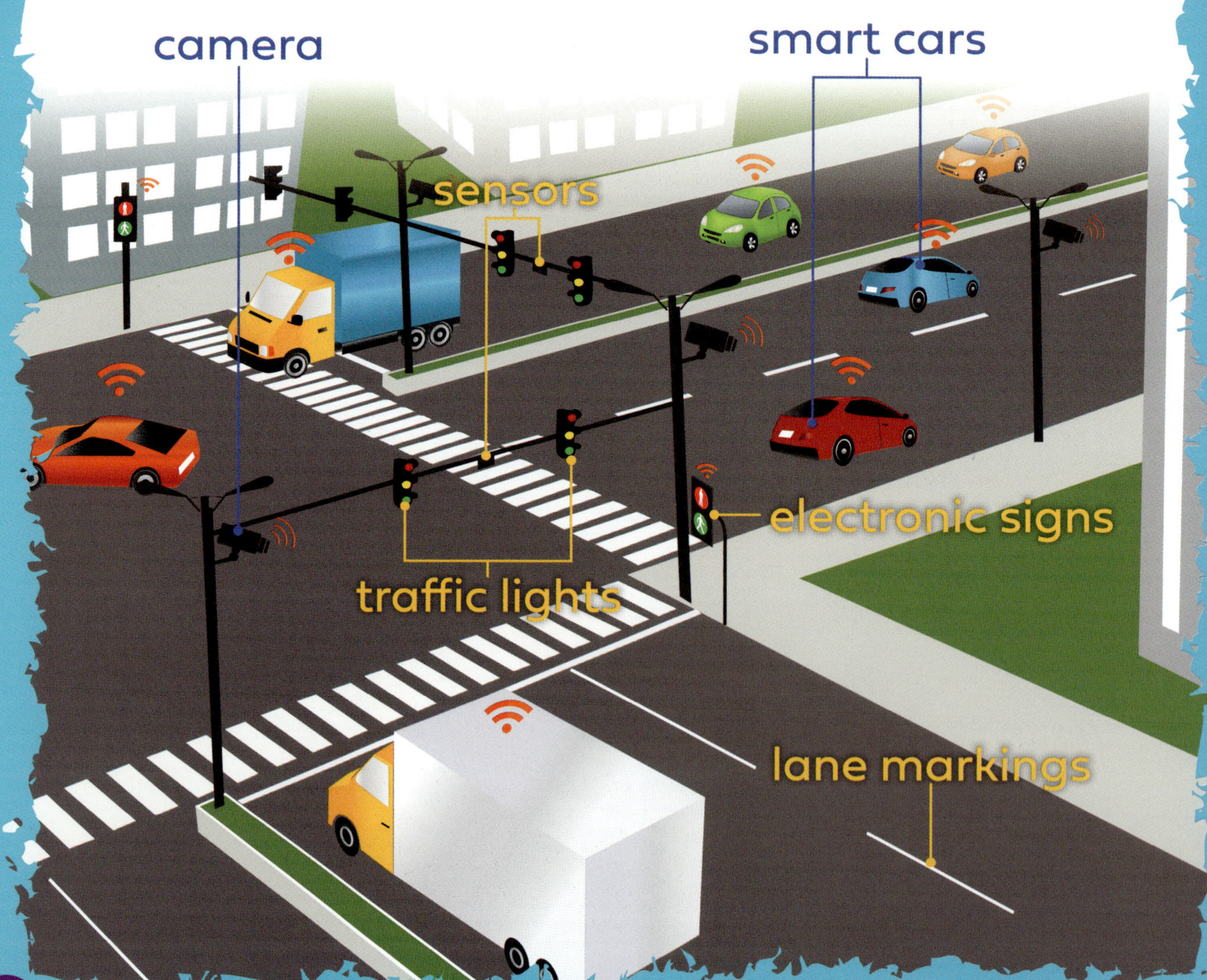

GLOSSARY

communicate (kuh-myoo-nih-kate) to share information

electronic (i-lek-trah-nik) something that uses electricity to work

features (fee-churz) special parts of something

sensors (sen-surz) devices that detect or measure something

signals (sig-nuhlz) things that send messages without using words

solar panels (soh-lur pan-uhlz) devices that capture energy from the sun to create electricity

technology (tek-nah-luh-jee) the use of science and engineering to do practical things

updated (up-day-ted) having the latest information

FURTHER READING

Lee, Maya. *Building Roads.* Steam Bookworks, 2023.

Rathburn, Betsy. *Self-Driving Cars.* Bellwether Media, 2021.

ON THE INTERNET

The Future of Roads: Smart Motorways
www.funkidslive.com/learn/roads/the-future-of-roads-smart-motorways/
Learn how smart roads make driving easier!

Roads and Streets
https://kids.britannica.com/students/article/roads-and-streets/276743
Britannica Kids describes the history of roads and highways and how they are built.

INDEX